ISSUES OF THE

Heart

Poetry by

SNOOK

AMARQUIS PUBLICATIONS

AMARQUIS PUBLICATIONS

AMARQUIS PUBLICATIONS
www.amarquispublications.com

For information about special discounts for bulk purchases, please contact
Amarquis Publications at amarquispublications@gmail.com

As a work of poetry, this book is a product of the author's imagination. Places,
incidents, events, names of persons, living or dead, are products of the author's
imagination.

Cover design: Indie Designz

First Amarquis Publications paperback edition May 2014
Printed in the United States of America
Library of Congress Control Number: 2014906899
ISBN-10: 978-0615996851
ISBN-13: 061599685X

Keep thy heart with all diligence; for out of it are the issues of life.

(Proverbs 4:23)

CONTENTS

I.

II.

III.

IV.

V.

VI.

VII.

VIII.

IX.

ISSUES OF THE Heart

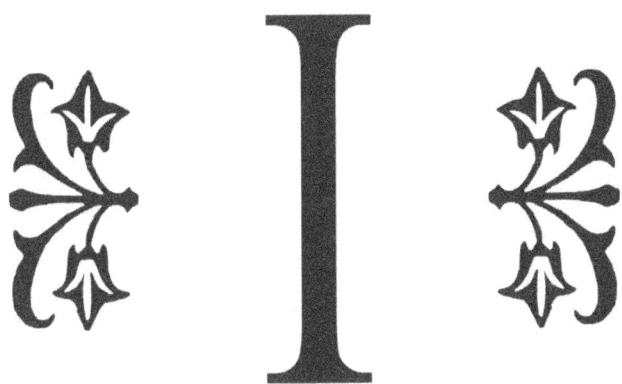

I

A Mother's Love

A little girl opens the refrigerator
To find what she know is there -- nothing.
Nothing but spoiled milk, hard cheese, and condiments . . .
But she has to eat something.

The last time she saw her mother,
She kissed her and headed out,
Telling her that she must stay asleep . . .
Alone, she wondered what that was all about.

Morning came and her mother was still gone.
She searched room to room looking for her,
Settling down on the couch,
Tears filling her eyes as her stomach ached.

Keys jingled outside the door,
Raising great excitement in the girl.
It's her mother with bags of food,
Wearing a smile and giving a twirl.

She kissed her daughter repeatedly,
Telling the child she loves her.
The girl realized her mother
Had not abandoned her.

Her mother walked six miles
To the store for food.
The time gone was all for her daughter,
Because in cabinets, now, was food.

Her mother didn't want her child to starve,
Doing what she had to do.
She knew their circumstances -- no car or family,
So she had to make do.

Later, the girl thought about her mother,
How she walked a great distance in the cold.
She didn't let transportation hinder her,
For she was amazed at someone so bold.

She wanted to be great like her mother,
Realizing obstacles are small.
They can be overcome with perseverance,
A life lesson learned for a child so small.

A Special Thanks

I am not one to boast
I strive for all of my goals
I will do whatever it takes to reach them
My mind goes in overdrive.

Planning out my strategy
Overcoming obstacles along the way
Setting guilt on the back burner
Pushing through any blockades.

I have accomplished much in this life
Motherhood, education, and careers.
But most of all, forgiveness
For those who have hurt me.

Forgiveness for those who lied on me,
Those who prayed for my downfall.
And forgiveness for those who failed to love me
As I have loved them.

With that, I take into consideration
Making myself happy
Never trying to please man
Bitterness is tossed away.

Pain buried deep in someone else's dark hole
Scars healed by the man above
I have a new walk and a new life
Full of accomplishments.

I have met my goals
And at times, exceeded
I took all of the pain and things I've learned
And turned them into my motivation.

I set out in this life to please only myself
Using my past as fuel to the fire
My hurt as a road map to success
Thanks for the help in making me who I am.

I say all of this with a loving heart
Always willing to take others on this journey
Always encouraging those willing to listen
At times, pulling up my sleeves to assist.

This I also have accomplished
So, I thank the naysayers
And defiled hearts for all of my accomplishments . . .
A special thanks to you.

Family

F is for making a **fool** out of me
A is for the **asinine** things you have done
M is for **motivation** that you have given me
I is for being an **idiot**
L is for the **lack** of love you have in your heart
And **Y** is something that I just don't understand.

II

Imperfect

As much as the edges
Are smoothed down
The more they curl
It's fine, just not perfect

A smile full of teeth
Not the brightest or the straightest
Good dental health
It's a smile, just not perfect

A full-figured woman
Curves and softness galore
Healthy and beautiful
This body is mine, just not perfect

Living life to the fullest
Although mistakes are made
I love me, I love my life
It's my life, just not perfect.

Black Is Beautiful

Chocolate, midnight, or cocoa
Skin ranges in colors alike
Love your black skin
Caramel, sunburst, and light.

Kinky, curly, straight, or bald
Hair textures so divine
Love your black hair
Black, brown, blonde, or red wine.

Hourglass, skinny, or thick-boned
Bodies in all shapes and sizes
Don't let your body define you
Tall, short, or average.

Don't let the numbers distract you
No kids, one, two, or three
Maybe four, five, or six
Be the best mother you can be.

Love your black children
Train them in the way they should go
Into men and women
One day they will grow.

Teach them how to love
How to survive
For nothing is given
For all is earned times five.

Single or married, be independent
Always save for that rainy day That
is sure to come anyway
Add value to your life every day.

Black is beautiful in its truest form
Black can shine
Your black is beautiful
I love mine.

It's yours
Live it
Love it
Embrace it.

*P*ower

Crawling on my hands and knees
Lip swollen as I taste blood.
The ache in my head signifies the damage
As usual, he let his anger flood.

Almost there, but not quite
Grabbing on to the wall to pull myself to my feet
My hand slips, almost sending me back down . . .
I knew this day was coming, but I'm scared of defeat.

I can hear him rummaging through the kitchen drawers
A fire is lit in me, knowing that the knife he seeks isn't there
The power he held over me will fail this time
My bloody shirt slips off my shoulders due to a tear.

No knife to my throat or the threat of death
No, not this time; it won't work
I'm almost there to the place of my power
Each time I wonder why I dated this jerk.

Footsteps quickly approach with heightened anger
I'm right there, but my ribs ache deeply with each breath
My left eye has swelled and blocked my vision
I know that I am one step closer to my death.

To my surprise, he has a knife
I slid my hand under the mattress
To his surprise, I have a gun
When he sees the gun, he is motionless.

He quickly backs away, dropping his knife
The metal slaps the floor and falls in my blood
My hand trembles, the gun unstable in my hand
He no longer appears to be that stud.

Get out or die, I say
The gun now pointed at his chest
He backs away slowly
I pray he would do what's best.

A boom echoes, speeding him up
Followed by me and my gun
'Never come back here,' I say
If I were him, I would run.

He's out the front door
With tears in his eyes
Don't cry now
One of us will die.

He leaves with no more fight
Now my life can begin
He is out my life forever
Never to be seen again.

III

Chances

Awaken by the sunshine
Beaming through curtains
The smell of coffee beans
Awaken with new burdens

Today is the first day
Of a new opportunity
Walking into the unknown
New challenges ahead

Fearlessness is a must
Determination is needed
Welcoming the challenges
That lie ahead

Chances are here for us to take
Take them at will
Chances may lead
Down new avenues

In life, we must take leaps
And sometimes bounds
Looking past the surface
To what's under, that's what matters

Once you are there
You would see
For in the end
It was all worth it.

The Fight

Life has its ups and downs
At times in our lives, we hold the crown
From infancy to death
Memories we collect
Through our eyes, we see things
We will never forget
Trials and tribulations are part of life
How we get through them
Gives us life
The choice is yours
How you choose to fight
Know that you are not alone

Free

Tall green grass tickles
On the back of my neck
Dark gray skies form above
I am about to get wet.

I close my eyes
As heavy cold raindrops
Fall one by one from the skies
Upon my unshielded body.

Slower at first, then faster
Raindrops heavier than before
I don't move as it covers me
I invite the coolness.

It's been a long day
This I can appreciate
I feel like a kid again
Rolling around in the wet grass.

The grass is wet and prickly
Pricking my back and sides.
I sit up to let the water drip down
My head, neck, and back.

I feel cool and clean
Then the rain stopped
I opened my eyes to gray skies
Making the way for blue skies.

I sit in amazement as the sun
Beams down warmth upon me
My body heats up
And the warmth begins to dry me.

A smile creeps across my face
As I lie back down
I am back in position
Resting again as the sun shines.

IV

Bodyquakes

Oh my, it feels so damn good
If this was a Richter scale
The last bodyquake would be a magnitude four
It sent me running towards the headboard
This one is a magnitude six
Damn, I can't take all of these licks
It made me run from the dick
Toes tingling, legs shaking
My back is arched so deeply
Moans escape my mouth
I bite my lip, almost too hard
As your tongue and suction
Sends me running again
I push back, but you are still attached
To my precious part
You have me in bizarre agony
As you suck and pull on my
Precious parts
It aches as another bodyquake is picked up
On the Richter scale, it reads a ten, but it's not finished
This one was off the charts
It couldn't be measured
I collapse, limbs numb
Legs too weak to move
Head spinning and heart pounding
Oh my, I feel so damn good.

Pleasurable Dreams

It's been awhile since I've been with a man
Only self-pleasure at my own hands
I dream of warmth between my legs
A tingle right there that makes me beg
For hardness pressed against my softness
An entry into my flesh that leaves me breathless
The face I imagine has strong manly features
I fantasize about this beautiful creature
We would make love so beautifully
A love that can't be matched to speak truthfully
We have our time for love and much more
I held back my feelings, afraid of what was in store
Wondering where our love could take us
What it would feel like to really trust
A man with my body and my soul
At times, I find myself being too bold
Then I shrink back into my shell
Admiring him from a distance . . . oh well
Maybe one day my dreams will come true
Until then, my pleasure is mine, I'll wait on you
Wait for you to finish your shift
And join me once again as I lift
These legs high above our heads
Tilting my bottom, making you beg
Calling out my name and fighting back

The urge to not go off track
We gaze into each other's eyes
Together we come, to my surprise
Just like in my dreams of us
You please me with no fuss.

V

Issues Of The Heart

Tears soak the pillow tonight
As I recall the hours before.
While I lay and wait for a response,
My advances are still ignored.

What is a girl to do?
He says that he loves me,
Yet I'm an option . . .
He opted out, I see.

When he wanted another,
He lied, schemed, and slithered.
When it comes to me,
It's every excuse, so love withers.

The love a woman has for a man is undying
If he loves her the same.
It's a powerful love that only a fool rejects,
But if the love isn't returned, who is to blame?

The love she has will soon fade away
And seek another's deserving heart.
With that said, it's time for me to go,
Love can't be forced; it is an art.

I am taking back my heart and my love
Or whatever is left, and grabbing on to it.
For I know there is a better love than what you are giving,
You can keep every bit of it.

When I find a safe place to store my love,
It will be too late to see eye to eye.
I look forward to what God has in store for my life,
But for me, this is bye.

The Second Wave

The first wave washed my soul away
I found it washed upon the sands.
You left me emotionally and physically
For this one, I wash my hands.

While I dwelled under falsehood all alone
You took my breath away.
Left me smiling through my pain
Yet you're begging me to stay.

Betrayal rocked me to my core
Leaving me empty and weak.
You said all the right things to get me to stay
But all that good shit lasted a week.

You did the right things to get me to believe
That our love was still true and pure.
During my thoughts of confusion and uncertainty
I was doing the right thing -- of this, I was sure.

I took the sand in my eyes, nose, and mouth
As the dust began to settle and the view became clear.
Now that the dust has settled
And there was no doubt the end was near.

I see the damage that has been done
My heart also riddled by the grains of sand.
Now you want to leave in search of your happiness
If I would have known this, I would have ran.

You think that you know what's best for me
So you bail out on me -- on us.
Directing me through traffic
I dare to jump on the first bus.

The second wave of pain hurt even greater
That pain took jabs at me, calling me a fool.
All that's left is eternal emptiness for what was
This relationship was better than school.

I learned how to love and how to hate
No matter how loyal you are.
If you choose a man that loves himself more
You wouldn't be able to get but so far.

Now I'm left after the second wave
With your last words professing your love for me.
Speaking of how good of a woman I am
Yet you are willing to let it be.

Most of all, how I am what every man wants in a woman
Yet you planned to desert me.
How does that equate
I am woman, I will survive, and you will see.

Low Tides

I can smell him on my skin,
Riding down the road.
No one knows the positions he had me in,
If a fly were on the wall, my truth would be told.

Chances are my man would never know
My phone was ringing between our kisses.
I didn't stop the passion, he didn't say no
Is this what he did with them other bitches?

Now I am back with the enemy,
The scent of sex made out of hate.
So what he hurt me?
No longer is my soul his to take.

I don't want you to go,
I don't want to be without you.
But the space we are in is too low,
Our truths ring too true.

Life isn't perfect, nor is it a game,
We try to push forward to better days.
But if I stay here, I will go insane,
'It will get better' is what they all say.

I can't do this anymore,
Please let me be free.
Being with you is a costly chore,
Don't look back, don't worry about me.

Let Me Love You

Is it a crime that I want to stay and do more this time
Nobody else is going to love you the way that I do
She will try to imitate me
Cooking for you, rubbing your back, and of course, lying on hers.

But me, I would love your heart, your mind, and the man you are
Never ever taking you for granted
By accepting the rations you may try to toss my way
Demanding the best out of and from you.

She is happy with whatever she gets
Only complaining of portion size, time, and the dick
Don't make a fool out yourself by flaunting an imitation
Because there's nothing like the real thing, baby.

You might let her try on my heels
But she sure can't walk in them; they're way too high
You see it, they see it, and she knows it
Let an independent, strong woman love you.

One who knows who she is, where she is going, and what she wants
Bringing passion, fire, and stability to an already powerful existence --
man.
Let the one who doesn't accept your disrespect, but demands your
respect, love you
The choice is clear who the real woman is, but the question is: are
you a real man?

VI

The Coffin

As I walk down the aisle
The carpet red and smooth
Passing mourners on the way
I have nothing to prove.

Slowly walking passed the pews
Mothers, fathers, brothers
Sisters, sons, and daughters
Too many faces to name them, so why bother?

I look straight ahead at the black and gold coffin
Seeing is believing, I dread the sight before me
The contents not yet visible
I walk with urgency so I can finally see.

A few feet away, my stomach in knots
Knees weak, but I must stand strong,
There is no one there to catch me
If I fall, I fall alone, here I don't belong.

The contents of the coffin more visible now
As I draw near and the choir becomes mute
I look back and all the faces are gone
Just an empty room with no décor to suit.

I rush towards the coffin,
With its top lifted high
To see myself deep in sleep
I smile and say goodbye.

Goodbye to the old
And in with the new
For days are short
In life, I must continue.

To grow and evolve
Into what He would have me to be
I shed no tears as I say these words,
I move away -- there is nothing else to see.

Death to my sins
Death to my old ways
Death to flesh
That's what the Word says.

Life In Death

How do I begin to say goodbye
The thought is too painful for me
I want -- no, I need to retain these memories
Of you in life; not in death.

How can life go on
Without you, my heart is heavy
My mind wanders to our past
And runs from thoughts of the future.

Why did you have to go
I know it's better where you are
But you are needed here with me
I don't blame you, but it's hard.

Now what do I do
Do I just lay you to rest
Go home and act like nothing has happened
Or do I give in to this pain I feel?

I know I must move on
Pick up where you left off
I know I must say goodbye
But it seems so final.

If I say goodbye
Then you will be forever gone
What if I hold on to you in this life
And never face the fact that death occurred?

This would make me much happier
Then I can go on with this life
I don't have to say goodbye
Because you will always be with me.

I will hold our memories safely in my mind
Store our love securely in my heart
Your beautiful face would forever paint my eyes
And because of this, I can finally say goodbye.

VII

On The Fast Track

On the fast track in life
He has NASCAR skills
Knowing when to break and when to press the gas
From this he can pay all his bills.

He don't get it honest
Always in them streets
Sleepin' all day, up all night
He stands on his own two feet.

Designer everything, all things blinged out
Counting more money than he can stash
Blinded by the game, he sees nothing else
But boy oh boy, it's about to be gone in a flash.

They're looking at him with his riches
Smiling, plotting, and seeping venom
Some are friends, family, and even foes
He doesn't see them as he picks up momentum.

It's too late when he finally runs off the track
Fighting for his life in familiar eyes
Hood crushed, fire ablaze, and he can't get out
He never saw it coming, taken by surprise.

In those moments, he has an epiphany
Seeing all of his past mistakes
Realizing nothing was worth it
Kicking himself for the blindness to what was at stake.

Believe and receive it
The streets have no love
Get out of that life
And into the arms of the One above.

A Fool's Paradise

Today's culture has shown the devil's hand
He holds hearts, queens, and kings.
Making us think backwards
Bad is good and good is bad things

Wake up, my people, and don't be fooled
By today's trends and hottest songs
For a day would come when we all are judged
Pick up your bible and read the book of Psalms.

Seek the truth so you are armed
With knowledge to navigate this life
There is instruction and motivation
Stop living in a fool's paradise.

VIII

My First Time

The sand squeezes between our toes
As we walk hand in hand.
As the wind blows,
We come upon a nice spot on the sand.

He pulls me close to his body,
Goes in for a kiss, and then another.
He lays me down, we see nobody . . .
He is one fine brother.

Our warm bodies on the cool sands
I think maybe we should finally go there.
The things I want to do to him may be banned
He takes off my top; my chest now bare.

The sound of the ocean waves and all
Heightens the sensations I feel.
We sink deeper, but he seems ten feet tall
I love this man -- he has skills.

He runs his tongue over parts of me
That I never knew could feel so good.
He moves far down, spreading my knees
Oh my, it feels so damn good.

Lost in his love, I go blind
Unaware of our surroundings.
He reads me, not missing a sign,
Entering gently, but soon, pounding.

Together, we touched the moon
Not once did I feel insecure.
The passion burned, ending too soon
He made me a woman, yet I'm still pure.

He Loves Me

I feel tingling in my bones
Every time he is near me
Butterflies invades my stomach
Every time he touches me.

When our bodies are close
In hot passionate love
Our souls pour into each other
As we make love.

We enter another realm
A place I've never been before
Feelings I've never felt
Thoughts I've never had before.

When we come down
My body and soul are at one
As our bodies settles down
We hold hands, our hearts beat as one.

When I heard the words 'I love you'
I drew in closer to him
To express the same
Meaning every word said to him.

When he asked for my hand
It was done so beautifully
When he placed the ring on my finger
The ring was designed so beautifully.

From the first time I saw him
I thought he was the one
When he confessed his love
I knew he was the one.

The Love Letter

At first, I had a heart of stone
Not allowing me to love
I found peace and happiness with you
We both have so many wounds -- some similar, some different.

You were an ear when I needed someone to listen
A shoulder to lean and cry on
Always there emotionally,
I found comfort in your arms and felt safe.

I knew that was the way that I wanted to always feel
We both shared things with each other that we have never shared
before
From day one, you accepted me -- good and bad
Not once did you judge or ridicule for being me.

Here we are, many years later with our family
You are what I needed then and what I need now
Throughout the years, we have endured trials
And tribulations that we have overcome together.

From this, I have learned that it takes the two of us
Together to continue to nurture this family
We are one and together we stand strong
You are my lover and my friend.

I love you for being you, for loving me
For being a father, and for your commitment to us
And most of all, I love you because of who you are . . .
Love always.

IX

Acknowledgements

Thanks to the readers for taking the time to read my first collection of poetry. Although, I have written poems numerous of times, this collection is dear to my heart. I can only hope that as a reader of such work, you are able to take something from these words.

A special thanks to those that offered their time and feedback during the writing process. A very special thanks to the editor J. Gomez and my designer Indie Designz for their talents. I look forward to sharing more of my poetry with you in the very near future.

Much love,

Snook

AMARQUIS PUBLICATIONS

presents

THE DAY THE WALLS CRIED

SNOOK

Coming soon from Amarquis Publications

www.ingramcontent.com/pod-product-compliance
Lightning Source LLC
Chambersburg PA
CBHW071847020426
42331CB00007B/1889